MARK F TARAGOWSKI

"Guardians Of Pet Wellness: Pet Insurance, A comprehensive Guide"

Common Health Issues in Pets

Contents

Preface

"Guardians of Pet wellness: **Pet Insurance**, A Comprehensive Guide" is your essential companion in navigating the world of pet insurance. From dogs and cats to exotic and unusual pets, this comprehensive guide demystifies the ins and outs of pet insurance, helping you protect and care for your cherished animal companions. Make informed decisions for their health and well-being.

Chapter 1: Introduction: Ensuring the Well-Being of Our Beloved Pets

P icture this: a warm, sunny day at the park, your loyal canine companion bounding joyfully through the grass, or the gentle purring of your feline friend as they curl up on your lap. For many of us, these moments of pure animal-human connection are nothing short of priceless. Our pets, whether they have fur, feathers, or scales, hold a unique place in our hearts, becoming cherished members of our families. They bring us boundless love, companionship, and an indescribable sense of fulfillment. In the tapestry of our lives, they are the threads that weave joy, laughter, and comfort.

As a pet owner myself, I understand the profound bond that can exist between humans and their animal companions. We share our home with Dash and Coco, two spirited dogs whose wagging tails and exuberant antics never fail to brighten even the gloomiest of days. And like you, we want nothing but the very best for them. We want to ensure that they live long, healthy, and happy lives, filled with love and care.

Yet, as any responsible pet owner knows, this journey comes with its own set of responsibilities, and among them, the vital task of safeguarding our pets' well-being, not only in terms of love and attention but also in terms of their health. It's a task that can bring immense joy, but it can also bring unexpected challenges, both emotionally and financially.

Imagine the distress of facing a sudden illness or injury in your pet, when you least expect it. The anxiety of rushing to the veterinary clinic, the uncertainty of diagnosis and treatment, and the weight of medical bills piling up. I've been there, and it's a scenario that no pet owner wishes to encounter. It's a moment when you'd give anything to make your pet well again, to see their tail wagging and their eyes bright with vitality. But the reality is, medical treatments for pets, like for humans, can be costly, and the expenses can escalate rapidly, leaving pet owners grappling with tough decisions.

Now, let's take a moment to consider something equally significant: the growing diversity in our choice of animal companions. Beyond the traditional dogs and cats, our lives are enriched by an array of unique pets - from exotic birds to reptiles, from small mammals to horses, and even rabbits, ferrets, guinea pigs, and more. These animals, each with their own special needs and potential health risks, are equally deserving of our love and care. They, too, deserve protection, both in terms of their physical health and our ability to provide the care they require.

It is within this intricate tapestry of pet ownership that the concept of pet insurance comes into focus. Pet insurance is not merely a financial product; it is a commitment to the well-being of our pets, a promise to stand by them in sickness and in health. It is a vital tool that empowers pet owners to provide the best possible care without the looming shadow of financial constraints. It offers peace of mind, a reassuring hand to hold when we face the unexpected twists and turns in our pets' health journeys.

But you might be wondering, what types of animals can be covered by pet insurance? The answer is wonderfully diverse.

Dogs: From the tiniest Chihuahuas to the largest Great Danes, pet insurance offers protection for dogs of all breeds and sizes.

Cats: Whether you have a playful Siamese or a serene Persian, feline friends are equally eligible for coverage.

Birds: Exotic birds like parrots, cockatiels, and macaws can be insured, ensuring their unique needs are met.

Small Mammals: Hamsters, rabbits, guinea pigs, and ferrets are all eligible for pet insurance to safeguard their health.

Reptiles: Lizards, turtles, and snakes can benefit from coverage for potential health issues.

Horses: Equine insurance is available for horse owners, providing support for these magnificent animals.

Other Exotic Pets: From iguanas to hedgehogs, even the most unconventional pets can find insurance tailored to their specific requirements.

The purpose of this book, "Pet Insurance: A Comprehensive Guide," is to be your compass in navigating this crucial aspect of pet ownership. It is a comprehensive resource designed to answer your questions, ease your concerns, and empower you to make informed decisions about pet insurance. We have structured this guide with your needs in mind, offering easy-to-access information, real-life examples, and expert insights to illuminate the path ahead.

Through the pages that follow, we will embark on a journey together, exploring the many facets of pet insurance. We will uncover the undeniable need for this invaluable protection, discussing the financial implications of pet ownership, and discovering how it can offer a lifeline when our pets face unforeseen health challenges. We will delve into the intricate workings of pet insurance, unraveling the various coverage options, and equipping you with the knowledge to choose the best plan for your furry or feathered friend. Moreover, we will celebrate the myriad benefits that pet insurance brings, from peace of mind to preventive care, and from coverage for accidents to support for chronic conditions.

But this book is not just for pet owners. It also serves as a valuable resource for insurance agents who seek to understand and guide their clients through the world of pet insurance. It is a bridge that connects the realms of pet care and insurance expertise, ensuring that those who safeguard our pets' health are armed with the knowledge to do so effectively.

As we journey through these pages, my hope is that you will not only find answers to your questions but also gain a deep appreciation for the profound impact that pet insurance can have on the lives of our beloved animals and those who care for them.

2

Chapter 2: Understanding Pet Medical Expenses and the Need for Insurance

In this chapter, we'll delve into the world of pet medical expenses and the crucial role that pet insurance plays in providing financial protection for your furry family members. As responsible pet owners, it's essential to comprehend the types of medical expenses you might encounter throughout your pet's life and how pet insurance can help mitigate these costs. Let's explore some common medical expenses pet owners encounter, along with estimated costs.

The Cost of Pet Care

Routine Check-ups and Preventive Care.

Routine veterinary visits are essential for maintaining your pet's overall health and catching potential issues early. These visits typically include:

Annual Check-Ups
Estimated Cost: $50 to $100 per visit.
Vaccinations
Estimated Cost: $15 to $40 per vaccine (may vary based on location and type of vaccine)
Dental Cleanings
Estimated Cost: $100 to $300, depending on the complexity and location
Flea and Tick Prevention
Estimated Cost: $20 to $60 per month for preventive products
Heart-worm Prevention
Estimated Cost: $5 to $15 per month for preventive medication
Emergency Clinic Visits
Estimated Cost: $500 to $1,500 or more, depending on the nature and severity of the emergency.

Accidents and sudden illnesses can occur when you least expect them. Emergency veterinary care may be required to address these critical situations. While the cost of emergency clinic visits can vary widely based on the specific nature and severity of the emergency, it's crucial to be financially prepared for these unexpected expenses.

Diagnostic Tests (X-rays, MRI, CT Scans)
Estimated Cost: $100 to $1,000 or more, depending on the

type and complexity of the tests.

Diagnostic tests are essential tools for veterinarians to accurately diagnose and monitor various health conditions in pets. These tests may include X-rays, MRI (Magnetic Resonance Imaging), and CT (Computed Tomography) scans. The costs associated with diagnostic tests can vary based on factors such as the type of test required and the complexity of the case. These tests are often necessary to evaluate conditions such as:

Bone Fractures: X-rays can reveal fractures and guide treatment decisions. The cost varies based on the number of images taken.

Soft Tissue Injuries: MRI and CT scans may be needed to assess soft tissue injuries, such as ligament tears or organ abnormalities.

Internal Organ Conditions: These tests are invaluable for diagnosing conditions affecting internal organs, such as tumors or blockages.

Neurological Disorders: MRI and CT scans help identify neurological issues and guide treatment plans.

Complex Surgeries: Surgical imaging ensures that surgeries are performed with precision, reducing potential complications.

It's important to consult with your veterinarian to determine which diagnostic tests are necessary for your pet's specific health concerns. The cost of these tests should be considered when planning for your pet's medical expenses.

Some common emergency situations for dogs include:

Trauma or Injury: Treatment for injuries like fractures, lacerations, or bite wounds can cost anywhere from $500 to

$5,000, depending on the extent of the injury and the need for surgery or hospitalization.

Gastric Dilatation-Volvulus (GDV or Bloat): This life-threatening condition may require emergency surgery, and costs can range from $1,500 to $7,500.

Seizures: Diagnostic tests and medications to manage seizures can accumulate costs of **$200 to $2,000 or more per year.**

Foreign Body Ingestion: Treatment to remove swallowed objects can cost $1,000 to $3,000, depending on the complexity of the case.

Anaphylactic Shock: Anaphylactic shock, often caused by severe allergic reactions, may require immediate treatment with medications like epinephrine. Costs can range from $500 to $1,500.

Intestinal Blockage: Surgery to address intestinal blockage can range from $1,000 to $5,000 or more, depending on the complexity and severity of the blockage.

Poisoning: Treatment for poisoning may involve hospital-ization, medications, and supportive care, with costs varying widely based on the toxin and treatment needed.

Heatstroke: Heatstroke treatment, including hospitalization and supportive care, can cost from $500 to $2,000, depending on the severity of the condition.

Common Cat Emergencies and Costs:

Urinary Blockage: Treatment for urinary blockages, a common issue in male cats, can cost $800 to $3,000, depending on the severity and need for hospitalization

Pancreatitis: Diagnosing and treating pancreatitis in cats may cost $500 to $2,000, including hospitalization and medications.

Hyperthyroidism: Lifelong management of hyperthyroidism with medications can add up to $300 to $1,200 per year.

Tooth Extractions: Dental procedures, such as tooth extractions due to dental disease, can range from $200 to $1,500.

Poisoning: Treatment for poisoning in cats may include hospitalization, medications, and supportive care, with costs varying based on the toxin and treatment needed.

Trauma: Cats can suffer injuries from falls or accidents, and treatment costs can vary significantly depending on the nature and extent of the trauma.

Emergencies can happen at any time, and being financially prepared for them is crucial to ensuring your pet receives timely and life-saving care. Pet insurance plays a significant role in providing this financial safety net, as it can help cover a significant portion of emergency veterinary expenses.

In the following chapters, we'll explore how pet insurance works, what it covers, and how to choose the right policy to ensure that you can provide the best care for your beloved furry companion, even in times of unexpected emergencies.

3

Chapter 3: How Pet Insurance Generally Works

I n this chapter, we will delve into the foundational principles of pet insurance. We will unravel the intricacies of policy types, deductibles, reimbursement rates, coverage options, policy exclusions, and the claims process. By the end of this chapter, you will possess the knowledge and confidence to make informed decisions about pet insurance, safeguarding your cherished companion's health and well-being.

Introduction: The Foundations of Pet Insurance

While the bond between pets and their owners is priceless, the financial aspects of pet care can be overwhelming. Pets, like humans, may encounter accidents, illnesses, or other unexpected health issues. Veterinary care is crucial for their well-being, but it often comes at a significant cost. This is where pet insurance steps in as a valuable ally, helping you navigate the complex terrain of pet healthcare expenses.

Pet insurance provides financial support when you need it most, ensuring that your pet receives the necessary medical attention without straining your budget. Whether your pet requires surgery, medication, diagnostic tests, or specialized treatments, having a pet insurance policy in place can make all the difference.

Section 1: The Basics of Pet Insurance
1.1 Policy Types
Pet insurance policies come in various types, each tailored to meet specific needs and preferences. At its core, pet insurance can be classified into three primary categories: accident-only

coverage, accident and illness coverage, and comprehensive coverage.

Accident-only coverage is designed to address injuries and accidents, offering financial protection if your pet encounters an unfortunate mishap. This type of policy is often the most budget-friendly option, providing essential coverage for unexpected events.

Accident and illness coverage extends the protection to include a broader range of medical conditions. With this policy, your pet is covered not only in the event of an accident but also when faced with illnesses, whether common or rare.

Comprehensive coverage represents the pinnacle of pet insurance protection. It encompasses both accidents and illnesses, ensuring that your pet receives comprehensive care in any medical scenario. While comprehensive coverage offers the most extensive protection, it typically comes with a higher premium cost.

Estimated Cost: Premiums for pet insurance policies can vary significantly based on factors such as the type of coverage, your pet's age, breed, and your geographical location. Typically, accident-only policies are the most affordable, while comprehensive coverage tends to be the most comprehensive and, consequently, more expensive.

1.2 Deductibles

Deductibles are a critical component of pet insurance policies. A deductible is the initial amount you are responsible for paying before your insurance coverage comes into effect. Deductibles can vary widely from policy to policy and significantly affect the overall cost of your coverage.

Estimated Cost: Deductibles typically range from $0 to $1,000 or more. Policies with lower deductibles often have higher monthly premiums, while policies with higher deductibles generally come with lower monthly premiums.

Choosing the appropriate deductible involves a balancing act between your monthly premium and your upfront out-of-pocket expenses. A lower deductible means that you will pay less when you file a claim but will likely have a higher monthly premium. Conversely, a higher deductible results in lower monthly premiums but requires you to cover more of the initial expenses when filing a claim.

1.3 Reimbursement Rates

Reimbursement rates are a fundamental aspect of pet insurance, directly impacting the portion of your eligible expenses that the insurance provider will cover after you've met your deductible.

Estimated Cost: Reimbursement rates typically range from 70% to 90% of eligible expenses, with some policies allowing you to select the reimbursement rate that aligns with your budget and coverage preferences.

For example, if you have a pet insurance policy with an 80% reimbursement rate and incur $1,000 in eligible veterinary expenses after fulfilling your deductible, the insurance provider will reimburse you $800, leaving you responsible for the remaining $200. The higher the reimbursement rate, the less you will need to pay out of pocket for your pet's medical care. However, policies with higher reimbursement rates often come with higher monthly premiums.

Section 2: Coverage Options
2.1 Common Inclusions

Pet insurance policies are designed to cover a wide range of medical expenses, ensuring that your pet receives the care it needs in times of illness or injury. These common inclusions encompass accidents, illnesses, surgeries, and diagnostic tests.

Estimated Cost: The coverage provided by pet insurance policies can vary depending on the type of policy and the specific insurance provider. The cost is typically built into the overall premium.

Accidents: Pet insurance policies generally cover the expenses associated with accidental injuries, whether they result from a fall, a traffic incident, or any other unforeseen event. Coverage may include veterinary examinations, diagnostic tests, surgeries, and follow-up care.

Illnesses: Pet insurance extends its protective umbrella to include a wide array of illnesses, ranging from common ailments like respiratory infections to more complex conditions such as diabetes or heart disease. Coverage often includes diagnostic tests, medications, treatments, and ongoing management.

Surgeries: In the event that your pet requires surgical intervention, pet insurance policies commonly cover the costs associated with various surgical procedures, whether they are routine, orthopedic, or soft tissue surgeries. This coverage ensures that your pet receives the necessary medical attention without creating a financial strain.

Diagnostic Tests: Accurate diagnosis is the cornerstone of effective veterinary care. Pet insurance policies typically cover the expenses related to diagnostic tests, including blood work, laboratory tests, imaging procedures (such as X-rays or ultrasounds), and more.

2.2 Additional Riders

Some pet insurance policies offer optional riders that can be added to your base policy to enhance coverage. These riders provide additional protection for specific aspects of your pet's health, such as wellness care, prescription medications, alternative therapies, and even coverage for lost pets.

Estimated Cost: Additional riders typically come at an extra cost, which can vary depending on the specific rider and the insurance provider. These additional riders are designed to allow pet owners to tailor their coverage to meet their pet's unique needs and their own preferences.

Wellness Care Rider: This rider focuses on preventive and routine healthcare measures for your pet. It often covers services such as vaccinations, annual check-ups, dental cleanings, and preventive medications like flea and tick preventatives. By adding this rider, you can ensure that your pet receives comprehensive wellness care.

Prescription Medication Rider: If your pet requires ongoing prescription medications for a chronic condition or a specific health issue, this rider can be immensely beneficial. It covers the cost of prescription drugs, ensuring that your pet has access to the necessary medications without breaking your budget.

Alternative Therapy Rider: Some pet owners prefer alternative therapies, such as acupuncture or chiropractic care, to complement their pet's conventional treatment plan. This rider can cover the expenses associated with these alternative therapies, allowing you to explore various treatment options.

Lost Pet Rider: Losing a pet can be a devastating experience. This rider can help mitigate the financial burden associated with advertising, rewards, and other costs incurred when searching for a lost pet. It provides peace of mind in case your pet goes missing.

By considering these additional riders, you can tailor your pet insurance policy to align with your pet's specific healthcare needs and your financial preferences. Each rider adds a layer of protection and can be a valuable addition to your base policy.

Section 3: Policy Exclusions

Understanding what pet insurance does not cover is as crucial as comprehending what it does cover. Policy exclusions are specific scenarios, conditions, or expenses that fall outside the scope of your insurance policy. Being aware of these exclusions allows you to manage your expectations and plan accordingly.

Estimated Cost: The costs associated with policy exclusions can vary, but they are typically not covered by your pet insurance policy.

Pre-Existing Conditions: Perhaps the most common exclusion in pet insurance policies is coverage for pre-existing conditions. Pre-existing conditions are health issues that existed before the start date of your pet's insurance policy. Since these conditions are known and documented, they are typically not covered. It's essential to enroll your pet in insurance while they are young and healthy to avoid pre-existing condition exclusions.

Waiting Periods: Most pet insurance policies have waiting periods before coverage becomes effective. During this waiting period, typically ranging from 7 to 30 days, your pet is not eligible for coverage. This period ensures that the policyholder does not enroll a sick pet with the intention of filing immediate claims.

Elective Procedures: Elective or cosmetic procedures, such as tail docking or ear cropping, are usually excluded from coverage. These procedures are not considered medically necessary and are often performed for breed standards or aesthetic reasons.

Breeding and Pregnancy-Related Costs: If you intend to breed your pet, it's essential to know that most pet insurance policies exclude coverage for breeding-related expenses, including prenatal and postnatal care, as well as the cost of breeding-related complications.

Certain Breeds and Conditions: Some insurance providers may have breed-specific exclusions or exclude coverage for specific medical conditions that are deemed high risk for certain breeds. These exclusions can vary from one insurance provider to another.

Understanding these exclusions is crucial to managing your expectations and planning for potential expenses that may not be covered by your pet insurance policy. While exclusions exist, pet insurance remains a valuable tool for mitigating many unforeseen medical costs and providing financial peace of mind.

Section 4: Filing Claims and Receiving Payments

Filing claims and receiving reimbursements are integral aspects of the pet insurance process. When your pet requires medical attention, navigating the claims process effectively ensures that you receive the financial assistance you need promptly.

Estimated Cost: There are typically no costs associated with filing claims, but reimbursement timelines can vary.

Submitting a Claim: When your pet receives medical care covered by your insurance policy, you will need to submit a claim to your insurance provider. This claim includes documentation of the veterinary services received, invoices, and any other required information.

Claim Review and Processing: Once your claim is submitted, the insurance provider will review and process it. This typically involves verifying that the services received are covered under your policy and calculating the eligible reimbursement amount.

Reimbursement Timeline: The timeline for receiving reimbursement can vary depending on the insurance provider. Some providers offer direct payment to the veterinarian, while others reimburse the policyholder after the claim is processed. It's essential to familiarize yourself with your insurance provider's specific reimbursement process and timeline.

Waiting Periods: Waiting periods also apply to the claims process, with some policies having waiting periods before certain conditions or treatments are covered. Be sure to understand these waiting periods to manage your expectations regarding when coverage will become effective.

Claims Deductibles: Remember that your deductible applies to each claim you file. After meeting your deductible, you will receive reimbursement for eligible expenses based on your chosen reimbursement rate.

Keeping thorough records and maintaining open communication with your veterinary provider and insurance company are essential when filing claims. It ensures a smooth claims process and timely reimbursement for covered expenses.

Section 5: Premium Determinants

Pet insurance premiums are the recurring payments you make to maintain your coverage. These premiums are influenced by several factors that affect the overall cost of your insurance policy.

Estimated Cost: Premiums for pet insurance can range from $20 to $100 or more per month, depending on various factors.

Pet's Age: The age of your pet plays a significant role in determining your premium. Younger pets typically have lower premiums, while older pets may have higher premiums due to the increased likelihood of age-related health issues.

Breed: Your pet's breed can also impact the premium. Certain breeds are prone to specific health conditions, which can affect the cost of coverage. For example, breeds predisposed to hip dysplasia may have higher premiums.

Location: Your geographical location can influence your pet insurance premium. The cost of veterinary care can vary from one region to another, affecting the overall cost of coverage.

Coverage Type: The type of coverage you choose directly impacts your premium. Comprehensive coverage tends to have higher premiums than accident-only coverage due to its broader scope.

Deductible Amount: The deductible you select affects your premium. Policies with lower deductibles often have higher premiums, while policies with higher deductibles come with lower monthly costs.

Reimbursement Rate: The reimbursement rate you choose is another premium determinant. Policies with higher reimbursement rates typically have higher premiums but result in lower out-of-pocket expenses when filing claims.

By understanding these factors, you can make informed decisions when selecting a pet insurance policy that aligns with your pet's needs and your budget. Keep in mind that while premiums are a recurring expense, pet insurance can provide significant financial assistance when unexpected medical bills arise.

Section 6: Choosing the Right Pet Insurance

Selecting the right pet insurance policy is a crucial decision that can significantly impact your pet's healthcare journey and your financial stability. To make an informed choice, consider the following tips and factors.

Estimated Cost: The right policy choice can save you money in the long run.

Evaluate Your Pet's Needs: Start by assessing your pet's age, breed, and health status. Understanding your pet's unique requirements will help you determine the type of coverage and additional riders that best suit their needs.

Research Insurance Providers: Explore different insurance providers, their policies, and customer reviews. Look for providers with a solid reputation for claim processing and customer

4

Chapter 4: Common Illnesses

Common Illnesses in Dogs:

Respiratory Infections

Respiratory infections, such as kennel cough and canine influenza, are prevalent concerns in dogs. These illnesses can spread easily in group settings or through contact with infected animals. Recognizing the symptoms, including coughing, sneezing, nasal discharge, and fever, is crucial. Seek prompt veterinary care to prevent the spread of infection and ensure your dog's recovery. In some cases, vaccinations are available to reduce the risk of these infections.

Skin Conditions

Skin problems like allergies, hot spots, and dermatitis are common in dogs. These conditions can lead to itching, discomfort, and even secondary infections. Understanding the underlying causes, such as food allergies, environmental allergens, or parasites, is essential. Your veterinarian can help diagnose the issue and recommend appropriate treatments, which may include dietary adjustments, medication, or specialized shampoos. Regular grooming and skin care can also contribute to your dog's overall skin health.

Gastrointestinal Issues

Digestive problems, including vomiting and diarrhea, are frequent in dogs. These issues can occur due to dietary indiscretion, food allergies, infections, or underlying medical conditions. Recognizing the signs of gastrointestinal distress, such as loss of appetite, abdominal discomfort, and changes in stool consistency, is vital. Managing these problems may involve temporary dietary changes, medication, or more extensive diagnostic workup. Always consult with your veterinarian to determine the cause and appropriate treatment for your dog's digestive health.

Dental Problems

Dental issues, such as gum disease and dental decay, are

prevalent among dogs. Neglecting oral hygiene can lead to discomfort, bad breath, and more severe health problems like tooth loss and infections. Learn how to maintain your dog's dental health through regular brushing, dental check-ups, and providing appropriate chew toys. Professional dental cleanings by your veterinarian may also be necessary to ensure your dog's teeth and gums remain healthy.

Common Illnesses in Cats:

Upper Respiratory Infections

Upper respiratory infections are common in cats, especially in multi-cat households or shelter environments. Conditions like feline herpesvirus and calicivirus can cause sneezing, congestion, eye discharge, and fever. Early detection and supportive care, including providing a warm and stress-free environment, are essential for a cat's recovery. In some cases, antiviral medications or antibiotics may be prescribed by your veterinarian to manage symptoms and prevent secondary infections.

Urinary Tract Issues

Cats are prone to urinary tract issues, including urinary tract infections (UTIs) and feline lower urinary tract disease (FLUTD). These conditions can cause discomfort, frequent urination, and litter box problems. Familiarize yourself with the signs, which may include straining to urinate and blood in the urine, and seek prompt veterinary care. Preventive measures, such as providing access to fresh water and a high-quality diet, can help maintain your cat's urinary health. Additionally, your veterinarian may recommend dietary changes or medications to manage or prevent these issues.

Dental Disease

Dental problems, such as periodontal disease and tooth decay, are common in cats. Neglecting oral health can lead to pain, difficulty eating, and more severe health problems. Discover the importance of dental care and how to maintain your cat's oral hygiene through regular brushing and dental check-ups. Professional dental cleanings performed by your veterinarian may also be necessary to address existing dental issues and prevent future complications.

Gastrointestinal Disorders

Gastrointestinal issues, like vomiting and diarrhea, can affect cats due to various factors, including dietary sensitivities, infections, or inflammatory conditions. Understanding the potential causes, such as dietary indiscretion or ingestion of foreign objects, is crucial. Recognizing the signs, such as lethargy and changes in appetite, and seeking veterinary care is essential for your cat's digestive well-being. Diagnostic tests, dietary changes, and medication may be recommended to address these issues.

By exploring these common illnesses and issues in dogs and cats, you will be better equipped to care for your beloved pets and ensure they lead healthy and happy lives. Each section provides insights into recognizing symptoms, seeking appropriate veterinary care, and implementing preventive measures to keep your furry companions in optimal health.

5

Chapter 5: Top Pet Health Insurance Providers

I n this chapter, we will introduce you to a sample of notable pet health insurance companies that have received recognition for their service.

Keeping in mind that the landscape of pet insurance is continually evolving. While I can't provide real-time rankings, I can introduce you to some prominent companies that were well-regarded as of my last update. Remember to conduct thorough research and consider your specific needs when choosing the right pet insurance provider for your beloved companion.

Pet health insurance plays a vital role in ensuring the well-being of our furry family members. As responsible pet owners, it's crucial to select a pet insurance provider that aligns with our pet's unique needs, our budget, and our preferences.

Trupanion www.trupanion.com

Trupanion is a well-established pet insurance provider known for its comprehensive coverage and straightforward policies. They offer a unique approach to pet insurance by providing coverage for eligible conditions with no payout limits. This means that your pet can receive continuous care for chronic or recurring conditions without worrying about annual or lifetime caps.

Trupanion's commitment to providing unlimited coverage has made it a popular choice among pet owners seeking peace of mind when it comes to their pet's health. They also offer a straightforward reimbursement process and a user-friendly online portal for managing your pet's policy.

Healthy Paws https://www.healthypawspetinsurance.co

m/

Healthy Paws consistently receives praise for its customer-friendly approach and high reimbursement rates. This pet insurance provider is known for its simplicity and transparency in policy offerings. They provide straightforward accident and illness coverage without the complexities of various add-ons or wellness plans.

One of the standout features of Healthy Paws is their fast claims processing, often completing reimbursements within a matter of days. With competitive reimbursement rates and a strong reputation for customer satisfaction, Healthy Paws remains a top choice for many pet owners.

Embrace https://www.embracepetinsurance.com/

Embrace is a pet insurance company that offers comprehensive coverage options and a reputation for excellent customer service. They provide a range of coverage options, including accident and illness coverage and wellness plans for preventive care.

Embrace's online portal simplifies policy management, and their claims process is known for being hassle-free. This provider stands out for its willingness to cover hereditary and congenital conditions, providing added peace of mind for pet owners concerned about genetic health issues.

Nationwide Pet Insurance: https//www.nationwidepetin surance.com

Nationwide Pet Insurance, formerly known as VFI, is one of

the most well-established names in the pet insurance industry. They offer various coverage options and have partnerships with a wide network of veterinarians and specialists.

One of Nationwide's notable features is their Whole Pet with Wellness plan, which combines comprehensive coverage for accidents, illnesses, and wellness care. Their longstanding presence and extensive network make them a preferred choice for many pet owners looking for familiarity and accessibility.

Pets Best https://www.petsbest.com/

Pets Best offers pet insurance policies with various deductible and reimbursement options, allowing pet owners to select the plan that best aligns with their preferences. Their user-friendly approach to pet insurance has garnered positive reviews.

Pets Best is particularly notable for its quick claims processing, ensuring that pet owners receive timely reimbursements for eligible expenses. Their range of coverage options makes it easy to find a plan that suits both your pet's needs and your budget.

Fetch Pet Insurance https://my.fetchpet.com
As well as coverage for accidents and illness, the Fetch plan also includes comprehensive dental coverage for illness and disease too.

While the pet health insurance landscape is diverse and continually evolving, these sample providers showcase some of the top companies known for their dedication to safeguarding the health of your beloved pets. Keep in mind that the right pet insurance provider for you will depend on your pet's unique needs, your budget, and your preferences.

Before making a decision, it's essential to research each provider thoroughly, read customer reviews, and compare policies to find the one that aligns best with your pet's well-being. Additionally, stay informed about the latest developments and rankings in the pet insurance industry, as new providers and offerings may emerge over time. Ultimately, the goal is to ensure that your cherished companion receives the best possible care while providing you with peace of mind in managing their healthcare expenses.

6

Chapter 6: "Paws & Claws Trivia: Test Your Pet Knowledge!"

1. Feline Friends:

Q: *How many whiskers does the average cat have?*

Answer:

A cat typically has 24 whiskers.

Q: What is the world record for the longest domestic cat ever recorded?

Answer:

The world record for the longest domestic cat is held by a Maine Coon named "Stewie," measuring 48.5 inches from the tip of his nose to the tip of his tail.

2. Canine Companions:

Q: Which breed is known as the "gentle giant" of the dog world?

Answer:

The Saint Bernard is often referred to as the "gentle giant."

Q: What is the smallest dog breed in the world?

Answer:

The Chihuahua holds the title for the smallest dog breed.

3. Animal Instincts:

Q: What is a group of cats called?

Answer:

group of cats is called a "clowder" or a "glaring."

Q: Which pet is known to have a "sixth sense" and can predict seizures in humans?

Answer:

Dogs are known for their ability to sense seizures and other medical conditions in humans.

4. Famous Pets:

Q: What was the name of the first dog in space?

Answer:

The first dog in space was named "Laika."

Q: Which U.S. president had a pet alligator in the White House?

Answer:

President John Quincy Adams had a pet alligator in the White House.

5. Pet Health and Behavior:

Q: What percentage of a cat's life is typically spent sleeping?

Answer:

Cats can spend up to 70% of their lives sleeping.

Q: How many taste buds does a cat have compared to a human?

Answer:

Cats have around 470 taste buds, while humans have thousands.

6. Odd and Unusual Pets:

Q: What is a "sugar glider," and where are they native to?

Answer:

A sugar glider is a small marsupial native to Australia, New Guinea, and Indonesia.

Q: What is a "capybara," and why is it a popular exotic pet in some regions?

Answer:

A capybara is the largest rodent in the world and is sometimes kept as a pet due to its gentle nature and social behavior.

7. Pet Insurance:

Q: Which country was the first to offer pet insurance to its citizens?

Answer:

Sweden was the first country to offer pet insurance to its citizens in the early 1890s.

Q: What is the most common reason pet owners file claims with pet insurance companies?

Answer:

Skin conditions and allergies are among the most common reasons for pet insurance claims.

8. Animal Records:

Q: What's the world record for the most tricks performed by a dog in one minute?

Answer:

The world record for the most tricks performed by a dog in one minute is 28, achieved by a Border Collie named "Smurf" in 2020.

Q: Which parrot holds the Guinness World Record for the largest vocabulary of any bird?

Answer:

A parrot named "Puck" holds the Guinness World Record for the largest vocabulary of any bird, with a vocabulary of over 1,700 words.

9. Pet Fun Facts:

Q: What is the only breed of dog that doesn't bark?

Answer:

Basenji is often referred to as the "barkless dog" because it produces unusual yodel-like sounds instead of typical barking.

Q: Which pet is known to have better night vision: cats or dogs?

Answer:

Cats are known to have better night vision than dogs due to their specialized retinas.

10. Animal Idioms:

Q: What does the phrase "raining cats and dogs" mean, and where did it originate?

Answer:

The phrase "raining cats and dogs" means heavy rain, and its origin is uncertain but possibly linked to old English idioms.

Q: What is the origin of the expression "sick as a dog"?

Answer:

The phrase "sick as a dog" is an idiom that has been in use for centuries, and its origin can be traced back to the 17th century. It is used to describe someone who is very ill or experiencing a severe illness.

7

Resources

merican Veterinary Medical Association:(AVMA): www.avma.org

AVMA provides extensive resources on pet health, including articles on common health issues and guidelines for responsible pet ownership.

American Animal Hospital Association (AAHA): www.aaha.org
AAHA offers guidelines for veterinary care standards and resources on pet health and wellness.

American Kennel Club: www.akc.org
Well Known and respected for its dedication to promoting the well being of dogs and maintains a registry of purebred dog breeds.

Forbes Advisor: www.forbes.com/advisor/pet-insurance/best-pet-insurance

Pet Health Network: www.pethealthnetwork.com

An online resource with articles, videos, and expert advice on pet health and wellness.

The American Pet Products Association (APPA): americanpet-products.org

APPA publishes industry statistics and trends related to pet ownership, including pet expenditures and the importance of pet insurance.

Association for Pet Loss and Bereavement (APLB):www.aplb.org

APLB provides resources for pet owners dealing with grief and loss, which can be relevant when discussing end-of-life care.

The North American Pet Health Insurance Association (NAPHIA):www.naphia.org

NAPHIA offers statistics and information about pet insurance, including consumer guides and explanations of insurance terminology.

The Humane Society of the United States (HSUS): www.humanesociety.org

HSUS advocates for animal welfare and provides resources on pet care and adoption.

Money.com; www.money.com/howmuchisitforanemergencypetvisit

OPENAI. (2023). CHATGPT(3.5) www.chat.openai.com

Your State's Veterinary Medical Association:
Your local veterinary association may have state-specific resources and guidelines for pet owners.

8

Conclusion

In the pages of "Pet Insurance: A Comprehensive Guide," we have embarked on a journey through the world of pet insurance—a vital resource for every responsible and caring pet owner. Throughout this book, we have explored the essential aspects of pet insurance, delving into the need for such coverage, the common medical expenses it can alleviate, and how it works. We've also introduced you to some of the top pet insurance providers known for their commitment to safeguarding your beloved companions' health.

At the heart of this guide lies the recognition that our pets are more than just animals; they are cherished members of our families, providing us with boundless love, companionship, and joy. As devoted pet owners ourselves, we understand the profound desire to offer our pets the best care and support throughout their lives.

The Need for Pet Insurance (Chapter 2) illuminated the financial impact of pet ownership, emphasizing the importance of being prepared for unexpected medical expenses. We explored the various types of animals that can be covered by pet insurance, ensuring that our guide is inclusive of a wide range of pets.

Chapter 3, "Common Medical Expenses," provided an in-depth look into the expenses pet owners commonly face, from routine check-ups and preventive care to emergencies and specialist treatments. By understanding these costs, pet owners can better appreciate the value of pet insurance in providing financial relief during challenging times.

In Chapter 4, "How Pet Insurance Generally Works," we demystified the mechanics of pet insurance, from policy options and coverage to additional riders and policy exclusions. Armed with this knowledge, readers are well-equipped to navigate the world of pet insurance and make informed decisions.

Chapter 5 delved into "Common Illnesses and Issues for Dogs and Cats," shedding light on the prevalent health concerns that our furry companions may encounter. By recognizing the signs and knowing when to seek veterinary care, pet owners can take proactive steps to ensure their pets' well-being.

In Chapter 6, we introduced a sample of top pet insurance providers, showcasing companies known for their dedication to safeguarding pets' health and providing peace of mind to pet owners. While these providers represent excellence in the industry, we emphasized the importance of researching and comparing options to find the perfect fit for your pet's unique needs.

As we conclude this comprehensive guide, we hope you have gained valuable insights into the world of pet insurance. Our aim was to empower pet owners to make informed decisions, ensuring that their pets receive the best possible care while managing healthcare expenses effectively.

May this guide serve as a valuable resource on your journey as a dedicated and loving pet owner. We wish you and your furry companions a lifetime filled with health, happiness, and cherished moments together.